Putting on a magic show

CONTENTS

Setting the scene

This book will show you how to put on a magic show.

You will need:

a costume . . .

a wizard's hat . . .

(1) *Cut out a shape like this from thin card. Make sure the bottom fits round your head.*

(2) *Join the sides together with tape to make a cone shape.*

(3) *Decorate the hat with cut-out paper shapes.*

a wand . . .

(1) Cut a piece of dowelling
30 cm long.

(2) Paint the piece of dowelling
black with white tips. Add
colourful shapes or stickers.

a table covered with a cloth . . .

and a magic spell.
Try this one:

Fizz, Whizz
Do the Bizz!

The stretching rope trick

You will need:

a piece of rope long enough to skip with.

Getting ready

① Before the show, take off your jumper or jacket.

② Hold the two ends of the rope in one hand.

③ Put your jumper or jacket back on. The rope should run up your sleeve and hang down your back.

④ If it hangs down below your jumper or jacket, tuck the loop end in your waistband.

The trick

⑤ Walk out in front of the **audience**.

⑥ Keep the hand with the rope behind your back.

⑦ Hold your other hand to your tummy and give a deep bow.

(8) Lift up the hand holding the rope. Tell the audience you want to skip with the rope so you need to make it longer.

(9) Wave the wand over the rope and say a spell. Then start pulling the rope. It will get longer and longer!

(10) Pull the whole rope out.

(11) Finish the trick by doing a few skips with it!

Pick any card

You will need:

a pack of cards.

Getting ready

① Ask a **volunteer** to shuffle the pack of cards.

② Pick up the pack. Fan the cards out.

③ Ask the volunteer to pick any card.

④ Close the pack.

The trick

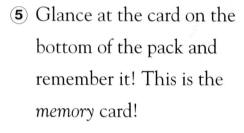

⑤ Glance at the card on the bottom of the pack and remember it! This is the *memory* card!

⑥ Put the pack face down. Ask the volunteer to put his or her card on top.

⑦ Cut the pack, putting the bottom half on the top half.

⑧ The *memory* card is now right on top of the volunteer's card.

9 Turn up the cards one by one.

10 When you turn up the *memory* card, the volunteer's card will be the next one.

A knotty problem

You will need:

a scarf.

① Fold your arms.

② Pick up the ends of the scarf.

③ Tie a knot in the scarf without letting go of the ends.

④ Then unfold your arms!

Tricky glasses

You will need:

three **identical** glasses.

Getting ready

① Stand the glasses as shown.

② Ask volunteers from the audience:

Can you turn all the glasses the right way up, turning two at a time, in exactly three moves?

The trick

③ Turn **A** and **B**.

④ Turn **A** and **C**.

⑤ Turn **A** and **B**.

A grand finale

Finish your show with the magic trick of the Wonderful Wiz!

You will need:

lots of colourful hankies . . .

three card cylinders like these . . .

33 cm   34 cm   26 cm

a wizard's hat, decorated
like the cylinders.

Getting ready

① Before the show begins, stand the biggest cylinder on end.

② Slot the other two cylinders inside it.

③ Fill the smallest cylinder with the hankies.

④ Tell the audience this story:

Once upon a time, the King had a dreadful cold. He sniffled and snuffled.

Nobody could help him.

Then a magician called the Wonderful Wiz came to court.

"Oh King," said the Wiz, "I cannot stop your sniffles. But with my magic cylinders I can make you feel better."

This is what he did . . .

The trick

⑤ Lift off the first cylinder. Put your arm through to show that it is empty.

⑥ Slot it back over the second cylinder.

⑦ Lift out the second cylinder. Show that it is empty.

⑧ Slot it back into the first cylinder.

⑨ Say a spell.

⑩ Reach into the cylinders.
Pull out lots of hankies!

⑪ Make a final bow, and
thank the audience.
Wait for the **applause**!

Glossary

applause   clapping from the audience

audience   people who come to watch a show

identical   exactly the same

volunteer   a member of the audience who offers to
                 help the magician

Index